THE PRAYERS OF THE PATRIARCHS

How Relationship Posture Impacts Our Prayers

Volume I

By
Apostle Darlyn C. Turner

DEDICATION

This book is dedicated to all of the patriarchs that have paved the way, and particularly the patriarch of my family—Anderson Hopson Sr., who introduced me to God, His word, and His presence

Copyright: 2008, 2021 Cedarlife Publishing All rights reserved.

The Prayers of the patriarchs By Apostle Darlyn C. Turner

Published by CedarLife Publishing

This book or parts thereof may not be reproduced in any form, stored in a retrieval system, or transmitted in any form by any means–electronic, mechanical, photocopy, recording, or otherwise— without prior consent or written permission of the author, except as provided by United States of America copyright law. Unless otherwise noted, all scripture quotations are taken from the King James Version of the bible.

2nd edition

Printed in the United States of America

ISBN 978-1-7335241-2-4

TABLE OF CONTENTS

DEDICATION — II

ACKNOWLEDGEMENTS — V

INTRODUCTION — VI

CHAPTER ONE COMMUNION WITH GOD — 1

CHAPTER TWO SUPERFICIAL PRAYER POSTURE — 12

CHAPTER THREE FORMAL (FORMING) PRAYER POSTURE — 18

CHAPTER FOUR SERVANTS PRAYER POSTURE — 23

CHAPTER FIVE FRIENDSHIP PRAYER POSTURE — 28

CHAPTER SIX SONSHIP PRAYER POSTURE — 31

CHAPTER SEVEN TALKING WITH GOD — 38

CHAPTER EIGHT WALKING WITH GOD — 45

CHAPTER NINE THE GOD OF OUR FATHERS — 52

CHAPTER TEN THE PRAYERS OF THE PATRIARCHS — 54

ABOUT THE AUTHOR — 72

ACKNOWLEDGEMENTS

Fathers are the givers of life and are critical in the emotional, spiritual and mental development of every human being. The role of fatherhood can never be underestimated, calculated or anticipated by any measurable means. It is only by the Spirit of God and the recording in heaven that the impact, impartation, influence and indelible mark that Fathers have can ever be known.

In a society now where many fathers are absent, we need more than ever for the fathers, the patriarchs, to cry out. Acknowledging every patriarch whose cry goes before His God for His family and humanity. We need you now more than ever!

INTRODUCTION

the prayers of the patriarchs...

Listen to me, you who pursue righteousness and who seek the Lord: Look to the rock from which you were cut and to the quarry from which you were hewn;

Look to Abraham, your father, and to Sarah, who gave you birth. When I called him he was but one and I blessed him and made him many. (Isaiah 51:1,2)

As we desire a closer walk with Jesus and want to know how to reach God in the dimension that transcends religion, formula, obligation, and duty to enter into the dimension of relationship that is simple, natural, perpetual, and powerful, we need to look back to the beginning of God's relationship with man, how God communicated with man, how man communicated with God and worshipped Him. I believe that as we do that, just as how we always need to understand the foundational principles of anything in order to operate authentically in its purpose, we need to take a closer look at "The Prayers of the Patriarchs."

CHAPTER ONE
COMMUNION WITH GOD

Let's first define prayer simply as an act of communion with God. We know that there are various types of "prayers" or different ways to commune, express, worship, or petition God. Paul even instructed us in Ephesians 6:10-18(KJV)

Finally, my brethren, be strong in the Lord, and in the power of his might. 11Put on the whole armour of God, that ye may be able to stand against the wiles of the devil. 12For we wrestle not against flesh and blood, but against principalities, against powers, against the rulers of the darkness of this world, against spiritual wickedness in high places. 13Wherefore take unto you the whole armour of God, that ye may be able to withstand in the evil day, and having done all, to stand. 14Stand therefore, having your loins girt about with truth, and having on the breastplate of righteousness; 15And your feet shod with the preparation of the gospel of peace; 16Above all, taking the shield of faith, wherewith ye shall be able to quench all the fiery darts of the wicked. 17And take the helmet of salvation, and the sword of the Spirit, which is the word of God: 18Praying always with all prayer and supplication in the Spirit, and watching thereunto with all perseverance and supplication for all saints; Paul challenges us to be strong in the Lord and gives a very important element in verse 18 that works alongside the "whole armor of God", "**praying always with all prayer and supplication…**"

There are all kinds of prayers, and many books on prayers and each one is necessary for us to be equipped to be able to pray "all prayer." There are prayers of supplication, intercessory prayers, prophetic prayers, warfare prayers…This book is not intended to emphasize another form of prayer, but to emphasize another "posture" or dimension of prayer, birthed strictly out of relationship, reverence, and rapport, which may include all of the above, but from a more intimate place of relationship which ultimately changes its "form".

Think about any relationship and how you progressed in your 'posture" of communication. When you first meet anyone, whether it is a boss, acquaintance, spouse, or a business relationship, the communication is usually extremely formal, rigid, and limited to specific boundaries. You are not sure what to say, how far you can go with certain subject matters, you may even address the person formally, by title or position only, which is an indication of the formality of the relationship. As the relationship grows, especially in intimate relationships, the walls of formality come down and you begin to communicate naturally with such ease and in such a way that you have lost consciousness of formalities (although not respect) and you converse solely on the strength of your relationship with that individual and the foundation of love, trust, and respect that has already been established.

This is the posture of prayer and intimacy that our fathers communicated with God. They did not search for specific phrases or deem any type of pontification any more powerful than the simple communication that exists between two people that have become one. Prayer from this dimension does not struggle with the limitless access of love, trust, protection, confidence, and security that are available for all of those who have a portion of this inheritance. This position of prayer is similar to a child that has been groomed and trained for his Father's business and has gotten to the place where the transference of authority now rests upon him as the successor. Because of the child's substantial time with his Father, the training and the obvious confidence the Father has exhibited towards his child that has been obedient and proven themselves as a true son, that child will operate at a different level of authority, power, favor, and even communication with their father because of the relationship, testing and training that has been endured. Similarly, relationship with God that includes transference of authority can only be achieved through intimacy, which gives access to power and favor that is always parallel to the level of submission.

Our fathers, the patriarchs of the bible, achieved this level of intimacy. Therefore, there was nothing off limits for discussion with the Creator and our forefathers. There was nothing off limits for God to discuss with them. God would not even plan to destroy Sodom and Gomorrah without first discussing it with the one who had this type of relationship with him—ABRAHAM. Stop and think about this for a moment. God, the creator of heaven and earth…is so reachable, humble and sensitive to us, his own creation, that he consults with those that are in relationship with Him. We all know that we have no right to be in on God's impending plans! However, not only did God consult Abraham, but Abraham had an obviously close enough relationship with his creator that he "reasoned" with Him: Genesis 18:16-28 (KJV)

16And the men rose up from thence, and looked toward Sodom: and Abraham went with them to bring them on the way. 17And the LORD said, Shall I hide from Abraham that thing which I do; 18Seeing that

Abraham shall surely become a great and mighty nation, and all the nations of the earth shall be blessed in him? 19For I know him, that he will command his children and his household after him, and they shall keep the way of the LORD, to do justice and judgment; that the LORD may bring upon Abraham that which he hath spoken of him. 20And the LORD said, Because the cry of Sodom and Gomorrah is great, and because their sin is very grievous; 21I will go down now, and see whether they have done altogether according to the cry of it, which is come unto me; and if not, I will know. 22And the men turned their faces from thence, and went toward Sodom: but Abraham stood yet before the LORD. 23And Abraham drew near, and said, Wilt thou also destroy the righteous with the wicked? 24Peradventure there be fifty righteous within the city: wilt thou also destroy and not spare the place for the fifty righteous that are therein? 25That be far from thee to do after this manner, to slay the righteous with the wicked: and that the righteous should be as the wicked, that be far from thee: Shall not the Judge of all the earth do right? 26And the LORD said, If I find in Sodom fifty righteous within the city, then I will spare all the place for their sakes. 27And Abraham answered and said, Behold now, I have taken upon me to speak unto the LORD, which am but dust and ashes: 28Peradventure there shall lack five of the fifty righteous: wilt thou destroy all the city for lack of five? And he said, If I find there forty and five, I will not destroy it.

Let's take a close look at the above exchange between God and Abraham. Firstly, God expressed the need to not hide what he was about to do from someone whom he had chosen and who had a tremendous call on their life. Abraham was commissioned to lead nations but even his influence on his own household impressed God, and God obviously did not want to leave someone that was close to him in the dark about his doings, even though He was God! Isn't that awesome that we know that God would not have us to be ignorant about anything that concerns us? He says in Amos 3:7 that "he would do nothing except he reveal it to his servant the prophet'. So, in prayer God does want to reveal secrets! **This is the real SECRET PLACE.** When you get to the place in God that he tells you His secrets, not just when you go to **"a"** place, but when you get to **"the"** place in him that he tells you what he will only reveal to His servants that know him, love him and obey Him!

What God revealed to Abraham was not even anything directly connected to him but as a Father of a nation, as one called to know God, as a witness in the earth it was important to God that Abraham knew what was going on. How much more does God want us to not be in shock about what is going on in our own household, communities and nation? If we would begin to expect to hear from God, and even the more, begin to ask God to reveal to us those things that are necessary for us to know because he said he would do nothing except he reveal it to his servants, we would not have to react, but we could, like Abraham intercede from our special place of influence with Him. Our intercession may not always have the desired result we prefer however, we can have understanding and peace, having done all to stand and being assured that we have done our part as watchmen on the wall.

I remember as a very young Christian, reading one of Kenneth Hagin Sr.'s books where he referenced that there was not one major event in his family (such as the death of loved ones, etc) that God did not reveal it to him and even warn him so that he could stand in the gap for his family and even bring warning if necessary. Although there were some whose end did not change, he had peace and comfort that God did not allow him to suffer through those times without first "consulting' with His servant. At that time, as a young Christian I reminded God of his word, that he was no respecter of persons and I asked God to do the same for me that he did for Kenneth Hagin. I asked God not to allow anything of any significance to transpire without consulting me, warning me, and/or giving me an opportunity to prepare, intercede, or warn those that it may involve.

I also prayed that I would be sensitive to hear him when he speaks. I can say God has honored that request.

"Father, we know that you don't do anything except you reveal it to your servants, whom you have chosen. We ask that as your servants (and friends) you show us anything, any calamity, any danger, or even opportunity for us to intervene, stand in the gap or receive your divine strategies for any given situation. We know that you desire for us to not be shaken, discouraged, distraught or dismayed so we give the Holy Spirit permission to awaken and alert us and we ask that we will hath an ear to hear what your Spirit is saying to us at all times, in Jesus' Name."

Have you ever reasoned with God? I know I have! Sometimes I think I missed my calling as a lawyer when I begin to speak to God about impending or probable events that may cause destruction or embarrassment to His kingdom and I plead with Him to not allow judgment to come strictly for HIS sake and not for the sake of the person, nation, or organization but for HIS sake and the sanctity of HIS word! God's exchange with Abraham in Gen 18:16-28 is a perfect example of intercessory prayer that is from a posture of relationship! When is that last time that you have heard an intercessor pray from this type of posture? This was not a prayer where Abraham had to raise his voice or give formal accolades; he simply in the strength of his relationship questioned God, in the character of His word. Have you ever had to reason with a friend, spouse or loved one? Do you recall that at the height of their anger and the apex of their wrath, it is with a meek and gentle voice and posture of your relationship with them that you are able to grab their ear and turn them from sure and sudden destruction! That is called intercession! Stepping in between life and death, love and hatred, judgment and mercy and giving a plea that will not be heard except the credibility of the "witness" can stand up to the judge as a respectable and reputable voice of reason and relationship.

Stop right now and listen to hear about any situation and or circumstance that God may be attempting to get your attention about, to warn you and others so that there will not be confusion or strife, but understanding and peace. Quiet yourself to hear what the spirit of the Lord is saying, and be willing to accept what sometimes is an inevitable event.

It is clear throughout scripture there was no need for formalities between God and our fathers. When Adam sinned, and abdicated the presence of God, just like a highly concerned parent searching for their beloved offspring, God did not wait for Adam to come to him, neither did he immediately shut Adam off from his presence, but God pursued Adam, and asked him "Where Art Thou?" Gen 3:9- 13 (KJV)

9And the LORD God called unto Adam, and said unto him, Where art thou? 10And he said, I heard thy voice in the garden, and I was afraid, because I was naked; and I hid myself. 11And he said, Who told thee that thou wast naked? Hast thou eaten of the tree, whereof I commanded thee that thou shouldest not eat? 12And the man said, The woman whom thou gavest to be with me, she gave me of the tree, and I did eat. 13And the LORD God said unto the woman, What is this that thou hast done? And the woman said, The serpent beguiled me, and I did eat.

You can see from the above exchange that their conversation was not formal, rigid, or full of salutations that did not fit that particular moment of conversation. God asked a direct question, Adam gave an excuse, God asked him another question, and Adam gave another excuse! I don't believe

you really have had real prayer, prayer that is dealing with the core of your character, redemptive communication and submission to the Father, until you can say that God told you to do something, or reminded you about your place in Him and you just gave Him an excuse! How can I say that? Because, if you say you haven't given God an excuse, either you really have not heard God in this dimension or you may still be communicating with God on a formal or superficial level.

God wants you to stop right now and revisit that directive that he gave you that you have continued to give him an excuse. It could be you need to forgive someone who sorely betrayed you, or to show mercy or love to someone you have deemed undeserving. Whatever it is, God desires for you to get rid of your excuse and obey! Repent, Forgive, and Obey, Release!

CHAPTER TWO
SUPERFICIAL PRAYER POSTURE

Matthew 6:7
But when ye pray, use not vain repetitions, as the heathen do: for they think that they shall be heard for their much speaking.

I would like to introduce five "postures" of communication that I believe exist in our walk with Christ. Each dimension of relationship reflects the realm from which we pray. Each of these positions of prayer is generally progressive with some vacillation between realms, based on the need. Think of these positions as being similar to our communication or roles that are varied with family or friends. Often, we have different "roles" that we play and interact with one another, and at times we must speak from the "posture" of a professional to our parents or loved ones, as opposed to just a friend or a daughter so that they can "hear" us, and quickly understand and respect that we are speaking from knowledge and training, and not just out of emotion or commitment to them from another aspect of relationship to them. Have you ever made a statement like this one, "I am not speaking to you as your daughter/son, I am providing advice to you that I would give anyone because what you are about to do does not make sense! Most of us have had moments as sons, daughters, spouses, etc., that we have had to use a different position (or posture) to gain access and favor where there may have been none.

The superficial level or posture of communication with God is one where there is no real relationship, just formalities, salutations, and slight familiarity. The prayer of the Pharisee in Luke 18 is a prime example of a Superficial Prayer: Luke 18:11-14 (KJV)

11 The Pharisee stood and prayed thus with himself, God, I thank thee, that I am not as other men are, extortioners, unjust, adulterers, or even as this publican. 12 I fast twice in the week, I give tithes of all that I possess. 13 And the publican, standing afar off, would not lift up so much as his eyes unto heaven, but smote upon his breast, saying, God be merciful to me a sinner. 14 I tell you, this man went down to his house justified rather than the other: for every one that exalteth himself shall be abased; and he that humbleth himself shall be exalted.

Superficial denotes a purely outward, shallow, not profound, thorough, or substantial relationship. Much like the bus driver you say hello to every morning for the last 15 years or the sister at church that you may engage in light conversation. You may speak to them daily, know their name, can identify them, and have interaction or contact with them, but there has been no true bonding or development of a solid relationship built upon trust, compassion, intimacy, or love. I believe many, who don't know God, many who are not even saved, communicate to God from this realm of "prayer".

I believe Cain may have been another example of one who spoke to God but had no real intention to serve him or obey him. His act of worship (giving) was an indication that he was only interested in surface or superficial worship. Let's take a look at the exchanges between God and Cain: Genesis 4:1-16 (KJV)

1 And Adam knew Eve his wife; and she conceived, and bare Cain, and said, I have gotten a man from the LORD. 2 And she again bare his brother Abel. And Abel was a keeper of sheep, but Cain was a tiller of the ground. 3 And in process of time it came to pass, that Cain brought of the fruit of the ground an offering unto the LORD. 4And Abel, he also brought of the firstlings of his flock and of the fat thereof. And

the LORD had respect unto Abel and to his offering: 5But unto Cain and to his offering he had not respect. And Cain was very wroth, and his countenance fell. 6And the LORD said unto Cain, Why art thou wroth? and why is thy countenance fallen? 7If thou doest well, shalt thou not be accepted? and if thou doest not well, sin lieth at the door. And unto thee shall be his desire, and thou shalt rule over him. 8And Cain talked with Abel his brother: and it came to pass, when they were in the field, that Cain rose up against Abel his brother, and slew him. 9And the LORD said unto Cain, Where is Abel thy brother? And he said, I know not: Am I my brother's keeper? 10And he said, What hast thou done? the voice of thy brother's blood crieth unto me from the ground. 11And now art thou cursed from the earth, which hath opened her mouth to receive thy brother's blood from thy hand; 12When thou tillest the ground, it shall not henceforth yield unto thee her strength; a fugitive and a vagabond shalt thou be in the earth. 13And Cain said unto the LORD, My punishment is greater than I can bear. 14Behold, thou hast driven me out this day from the face of the earth; and from thy face shall I be hid; and I shall be a fugitive and a vagabond in the earth; and it shall come to pass, that every one that findeth me shall slay me. 15And the LORD said unto him, Therefore whosoever slayeth Cain, vengeance shall be taken on him sevenfold. And the LORD set a mark upon Cain, lest any finding him should kill him. 16And Cain went out from the presence of the LORD, and dwelt in the land of Nod, on the east of Eden.

We can see from the above exchange some very key points. We know that Cain was only interested in doing the minimal sacrifice, the minimal worship, thus maintaining a "superficial" or surface level of worship and obedience to God. We also know that God was not pleased with this level of devotion and was quick to express his displeasure. Now what is interesting in the exchange between God and Cain is that there is an implication that Cain ignored God's displeasure and advice. He failed to respond to any of God's warnings or advice, probably because he already had his mind made up how he wanted to serve God.

So, we can see in verse 5 that God had to have communicated to Cain his dissatisfaction with his offering, because Cain became "wroth," and his countenance fail. However, he did not even ask God any questions or seek retribution. God in his mercy, despite Cain's pride, gave him a way of escape and a warning letting him know all he had to do was change his sacrifice, but if he did not change, he let him know "sin lieth at the door" but it was all his choice! Cain still did not respond to God but took everything out on his brother. After slaying his brother Abel, God asked him about the whereabouts of his brother, and he gave the now infamous answer, "Am I my brother's keeper." Then after hearing God's punishment he let God know that it was more than he could bear.

Isn't it a shame that many of us, just like Cain, do not communicate with God in the stages where it is needed most? God is always trying to help us, correct us, and protect us from destruction and judgment but when we really are not postured for submission and obedience we often do not talk to God until it is too late and the judgment has been set. God is always attempting to warn us and save us from destruction. This posture of prayer is most identifiable by its tendency to be prevalent only in times of trouble and distress. **Those who communicate from this place usually communicate when they are forced to because of the circumstances in their life that they have created because of their failure to hear God's voice along the way.**

CHAPTER THREE
FORMAL (FORMING)
PRAYER POSTURE

LUKE 11:1
"...Lord, teach us to pray, as John also taught his disciples."

A formal posture of prayer is a place of non-familiarity with God and His voice that you rely mostly on outward direction (spiritual leaders, prayer books, etc), and your perception of Him and what he wants from you. At this point, the relationship is still forming and the interaction has not been frequent or effective enough to form the type of camaraderie, vulnerability, and nakedness that leads to the Holy Spirit having access to deal with you in every place that is necessary. Much training in prayer is done at this level, so that we can advance to the place where we can serve out of knowledge and not just zeal. This is the stage where we learn intercessory prayers, warfare prayers, how to pray for the nations, prophetic prayers etc...This formal stage helps us to take our place as servants, fit for the master's use. The formal posture is a necessary step in our progression of learning how to be effective in prayer. However, just like anyone still in "on the job training", this level of relationship has not reached the maturity, confidence, and assurance that is obvious when two have become one. It takes this learning stage of prayer and communion to develop a rhythm, trust and bond of peace that only develops through communication, intimacy, trust, and truth, which does take time to manifest. The bible gives us a glimpse in the life of a man of God's beginning place of prayer, to let us know that although he became one that "not one word fell to the ground", Samuel did not even know God's voice until his mentor, Eli helped to train him to hear God and respond.

1 Samuel 3:1-10

1And the child Samuel ministered unto the LORD before Eli. And the word of the LORD was precious in those days; there was no open vision. 2And it came to pass at that time, when Eli was laid down in his place, and his eyes began to wax dim, that he could not see; 3And ere the lamp of God went out in the temple of the LORD, where the ark of God was, and Samuel was laid down to sleep; 4That the LORD called Samuel: and he answered, Here am I. 5And he ran unto Eli, and said, Here am I; for thou calledst me.

And he said, I called not; lie down again. And he went and lay down. 6And the LORD called yet again, Samuel. And Samuel arose and went to Eli, and said, Here am I; for thou didst call me. And he answered, I called not, my son; lie down again. 7Now Samuel did not yet know the LORD, neither was the word of the LORD yet revealed unto him. 8And the LORD called Samuel again the third time. And he arose and went to Eli, and said, Here am I; for thou didst call me. And Eli perceived that the LORD had called the child. 9Therefore Eli said unto Samuel, Go, lie down: and it shall be, if he call thee, that thou shalt say, Speak, LORD; for thy servant heareth. So Samuel went and lay down in his place. 10And the LORD came, and stood, and called as at other times, Samuel, Samuel. Then Samuel answered, Speak; for thy servant heareth.

Samuel is a powerful example of the progression that we must all make in getting to know God. It is not an instantaneous relationship, although we are instantly saved, redeemed and set free from eternal damnation. It still takes time for our relationship with the Lord to develop, for us to be converted, and for us to really be able to distinguish HIS voice from others, and to come to know HIM. We can see with Samuel, in verse 1 that he was "ministering before the Lord" under Eli but verse 7 is clear he "did not yet know the Lord"! WHEW! That is something to stop and think about right here. I might get in trouble on this one, but I declare there are many on national circuits, Christian television, and selling millions of books that are ministering before the Lord but don't know HIM! How can I say that? Because to know Him is to fear Him, to know Him is to love his children, and to obey his commandments.

Samuel was raised in the church, had a great testimony, his mother had turned him over to the man of God, he was dedicated to God, etc, but that did not qualify him to know God until he took the steps to develop his relationship and spent the time in prayer, the word, consecration, and conversation with his maker to be able to know him for himself. I think too often in the body of Christ we put people up too soon, with testimonies like Samuel, and although we celebrate the testimony, we don't always seem to discern whether they have really come to know God, which accounts for many of our disgraces and failures in the body of Christ, that impact us all. Look at how Samuel's relationship with God developed according to 1 Samuel 3:19- 21 (KJV)

19And Samuel grew, and the LORD was with him, and did let none of his words fall to the ground. 20And all Israel from Dan even to Beersheba knew that Samuel was established to be a prophet of the LORD. 21And the LORD appeared again in Shiloh:

for the LORD revealed himself to Samuel in Shiloh by the word of the LORD.

So, Samuel's continual communication and interaction in God's presence, and particularly through the entrance of the word of God, caused Samuel to grow in Him and for God to back up his words and not allow them to fall! As we also develop our prayer to be in alignment with God's word, our words cannot come back void!

It is evident that Samuel went from a formal posture to a posture of a servant, soon recognized by both God and man.

Formalities exist only between those whose relationship has not reached the level of intimacy where they are no longer necessary.

CHAPTER FOUR
SERVANTS PRAYER POSTURE

Psalm 27:9

Hide not that face far from me; put not thy servant away in anger: thou hast been my help; leave me not, neither forsakes me, O God of my salvation

    The servant's posture of prayer is where we know God, serve Him, and appreciate Him as our Lord and Savior from a place of service. When you really become a servant at heart there is an innate desire to please your Master so you are seeking Him, like never before because you so desire to please him and to hear him say, "Well done, thy Good and faithful servant". This is the place, much as a servant has come to know his master, where you can anticipate the voice and desires of your master. A servant knows the language, culture, and movements of his master, which enhances their ability to serve. A servant's posture is more attuned to the master's needs at any given moment than one that may still be growing in God and praying out of books or other formulas. A servant is so up close and personal that they pray from a position that not many people can see. I believe many spouses of leaders can identify with this posture, as entire families are called whenever leaders have a significant mandate on their lives. The spouse that is not in the limelight must then serve the needs, causes, and vision in a way others may not imagine. While even the entire world, may be praying for their spouse's vision, agendas, ministry, etc...only those that serve them can pray very specifically and uniquely to some of the real critical issues that may plaque the life of a public figure.

Much like the servant girl, who served Naaman's wife and obviously wanted to see Naaman healed, servants have been strategically placed next to men and women of position and power, in order to impact change in their lives and to provide protection in prayer. Often, it is only the servant that can see the root issues or critical needs of a leader, nation, or community. This posture is inherent in the life of our savior who was "touched" with our infirmities and temptations. Servants have a sensitivity that sometimes a formal or religious posture cannot even imagine. It takes this posture many times to forgive those who may have sinned and to be like Jesus was when the woman was caught in adultery. His posture of a servant would not allow condemnation, but to ask, "Let he who has no sin to cast the first stone." True servants are guided by compassion, forgiveness, and love and therefore their prayers and expectations are of redemption, conquest, and victory.

I believe David has provided many samples of this posture, although he vacillated between the posture of both servant and friend (which we will continue to vacillate at times through various postures). Just as the servant is well aware of what pleases his master, he is just as much aware of what displeases his master. Let's take a look at this dimension as demonstrated in the prayers of David soon after Nathan exposed David's sin, David's ultimate concern was his not his position as King, what other people thought, or what he stood to lose, David's focus as a servant of the most high God was always staying in right relationship with his master.

PSALM 51:1-19

1Have mercy upon me, O God, according to thy lovingkindness: according unto the multitude of thy tender mercies blot out my transgressions. 2Wash me throughly from mine iniquity, and cleanse me from my sin. 3For I acknowledge my transgressions: and my sin is ever before me.

4 Against thee, thee only, have I sinned, and done this evil in thy sight: that thou mightest be justified when thou speakest, and be clear when thou judgest. 5 Behold, I was shapen in iniquity; and in sin did my mother conceive me. 6 Behold, thou desirest truth in the inward parts: and in the hidden part thou shalt make me to know wisdom. 7 Purge me with hyssop, and I shall be clean: wash me, and I shall be whiter than snow. 8 Make me to hear joy and gladness; that the bones which thou hast broken may rejoice. 9 Hide thy face from my sins, and blot out all mine iniquities. 10 Create in me a clean heart, O God; and renew a right spirit within me. 11 Cast me not away from thy presence; and take not thy holy spirit from me. 12 Restore unto me the joy of thy salvation; and uphold me with thy free spirit. 13 Then will I teach transgressors thy ways; and sinners shall be converted unto thee. 14 Deliver me from bloodguiltiness, O God, thou God of my salvation: and my tongue shall sing aloud of thy righteousness. 15 O Lord, open thou my lips; and my mouth shall shew forth thy praise. 16 For thou desirest not sacrifice; else would I give it: thou delightest not in burnt offering. 17 The sacrifices of God are a broken spirit: a broken and a contrite heart, O God, thou wilt not despise. 18 Do good in thy good pleasure unto Zion: build thou the walls of Jerusalem. 19 Then shalt thou be pleased with the sacrifices of righteousness, with burnt offering and whole burnt

offering: then shall they offer bullocks upon thine altar.

Servant communication is best described as being expressions of humility, submission, recognizance, debt, and acknowledgment of their master while providing supplication and intercession for oneself, others, nations, communities, or causes. David's verbiage in psalm 51 provides an obvious knowledge of the character of God reminding Him of his "unfailing love" and citing what He desires, "a broken spirit; a broken and contrite heart." David prays from a position of relationship that comes from knowledge and places him at an advantage in knowing God's mercy, what he desires, and what he requires. Even though there are other dimensions to converse with God, this dimension is everlasting, as we always remain servants and I believe this is why David was described as "a man after God's own heart", as this tends to be the place of utmost sensitivity to God, his needs, and his righteousness.

CHAPTER FIVE
FRIENDSHIP PRAYER POSTURE

GENESIS 17:3-4

And Abram fell on his face: and God talked with him saying, As for me, behold, my covenant is with thee, and thou shalt be a father of many nations.

The "friend" posture of prayer is the dimension of communication with God that we have become qualified to be confided in by God. John 15 says:

1 I am the true vine, and my Father is the husbandman. 2 Every branch in me that beareth not fruit he taketh away: and every branch that beareth fruit, he purgeth it, that it may bring forth more fruit. 3 Now ye are clean through the word which I have spoken unto you. 4 Abide in me, and I in you. As the branch cannot bear fruit of itself, except it abide in the vine; no more can ye, except ye abide in me. 5 I am the vine, ye are the branches: He that abideth in

me, and I in him, the same bringeth forth much fruit: for without me ye can do nothing. 6 If a man abide not in me, he is cast forth as a branch, and is withered; and men gather them, and cast them into the fire, and they are burned. 7 If ye abide in me, and my words abide in you, ye shall ask what ye will, and it shall be done unto you. 8 Herein is my Father glorified, that ye bear much fruit; so shall ye be my disciples. 9 As the Father hath loved me, so have I loved you: continue ye in my love. 10 If ye keep my commandments, ye shall abide in my love; even as I have kept my Father's commandments, and abide in his love. 11 These things have I spoken unto you, that my joy might remain in you, and that your joy might be full. 12 This is my commandment, That ye love one another, as I have loved you. 13 Greater love hath no man than this, that a man lay down his life for his friends. 14 Ye are my friends, if ye do whatsoever I command you. 15 Henceforth I call you not servants; for the servant knoweth not what his lord doeth: but I have called you friends; for all things that I have heard of my Father I have made known unto you.

God's desire is that we be no longer servants but friends! So God wants us to "graduate" from a servant mentality and communication with him to a friendship mentality and communication! How intimate is a master with his servants? Can you see the difference in the dimension of conversation, intimacy, and formality that exists between a master and his servant, versus a master and his friend? However, it is clear that you don't just become a friend of God because you talk to him every day. God makes it clear that his friends are those who obey him! We do not become God's friend just because we pray. As we now know, you can pray or communicate with God without ever obeying His voice. God is clear that he reveals another dimension of himself to those who obey Him. There is information, understanding, and revelation that only "friends" will know. The Body of Christ must wake up and see that God wants some friends! Make up your mind today to truly become a "friend" of God by becoming obedient, remaining in love, and being willing to do whatever God commands.

CHAPTER SIX SONSHIP PRAYER POSTURE

John 17:1

"...glorify thy Son, that thy Son also may glorify thee"

The highest dimension or posture is the posture of "son". This is the dimension that Jesus dwelt in from beginning to end, being the epitome of this dimension, functioning in full confidence, authority, submission, power, and likeness of the father. Jesus' prayer in John 17 is an example of the authoritative position of sons. We have actually probably inappropriately titled "The Lord's Prayer" found in Matt 6:9-13. This prayer was really not our Lord's Prayer; this is the prayer that he used to train the disciples how to pray. It probably would more appropriately be called, "The Disciples Prayer." Let's take a look at our Lord's Prayer found in John 17:1-26

The Prayers of the Patriarchs

1These words spake Jesus, and lifted up his eyes to heaven, and said, Father, the hour is come; glorify thy Son, that thy Son also may glorify thee: 2As thou hast given him power over all flesh, that he should give eternal life to as many as thou hast given him. 3And this is life eternal, that they might know thee the only true God, and Jesus Christ, whom thou hast sent. 4I have glorified thee on the earth: I have finished the work which thou gavest me to do. 5And now, O Father, glorify thou me with thine own self with the glory which I had with thee before the world was. 6I have manifested thy name unto the men which thou gavest me out of the world: thine they were, and thou gavest them me; and they have kept thy word. 7Now they have known that all things whatsoever thou hast given me are of thee. 8For I have given unto them the words which thou gavest me; and they have received them, and have known surely that I came out from thee, and they have believed that thou didst send me. 9I pray for them: I pray not for the world, but for them which thou hast given me; for they are thine. 10And all mine are thine, and thine are mine; and I am glorified in them. 11And now I am no more in the world, but these are in the world, and I come to thee. Holy Father, keep through thine own name those whom thou hast given me, that they may be one, as we are. 12While I was with them in the world, I kept them in thy name: those that thou gavest me I have kept, and none of them is lost, but the son of perdition;

that the scripture might be fulfilled. 13And now come I to thee; and these things I speak in the world, that they might have my joy fulfilled in themselves. 14I have given them thy word; and the world hath hated them, because they are not of the world, even as I am not of the world. 15I pray not that thou shouldest take them out of the world, but that thou shouldest keep them from the evil. 16They are not of the world, even as I am not of the world. 17Sanctify them through thy truth: thy word is truth. 18As thou hast sent me into the world, even so have I also sent them into the world. 19And for their sakes I sanctify myself, that they also might be sanctified through the truth. 20Neither pray I for these alone, but for them also which shall believe on me through their word; 21That they all may be one; as thou, Father, art in me, and I in thee, that they also may be one in us: that the world may believe that thou hast sent me. 22And the glory which thou gavest me I have given them; that they may be one, even as we are one: 23I in them, and thou in me, that they may be made perfect in one; and that the world may know that thou hast sent me, and hast loved them, as thou hast loved me. 24Father, I will that they also, whom thou hast given me, be with me where I am; that they may behold my glory, which thou hast given me: for thou lovedst me before the foundation of the world. 25O righteous Father, the world hath not known thee: but I have known thee, and these have known that thou hast sent me. 26And

I have declared unto them thy name, and will declare it: that the love wherewith thou hast loved me may be in them, and I in them.

This dimension warrants our full attention to the confidence, knowledge, relationship, honor, and focus on purpose that sonship brings in communication with the Father. We know from the beginning, Jesus "was about his Father's business" and his identity, image, and initiatives were never outside of his relationship as the son. When we get to the place that everything we do and say is in alignment with the image of our Father, we have begun to walk as sons and not just even friends.

There are several things to point out in Jesus' prayer from His position of the son, the first one being that he was aware of the timing of the Father and knew that his time had come. How much headache and heartache would we avoid if we really knew the timing of our father, even in the times of suffering and were able to ask for Him to glorify us so that he could be glorified? Have you been afraid to asked God to glorify you? We need to be glorified so that He can be glorified! Only a son can ask for the glory of his father, only a son can have the audacity to request such a thing. Let's stop and pray right now...

Father, glorify me in every situation that faces me right now, so that you, my heavenly Father, will be glorified!

Jesus knew the authority granted to him and why it was granted (verse 2), he knew he was sent (verse 3), and he was confident that he had completed his task and in that had glorified God (verse 4). Jesus as son continually acknowledged that everything he had done, everyone he was sent to, everything attached to him was only through his sonship relationship to the father (verses 6-10). As much as Jesus knew all he had was from God, he was just as confident that all God had was his. Jesus was also fully aware that there were those who did not know his father, but their acceptance of him was the gateway to knowing the Father. Jesus knew there was glory attached to his life but he knew that all glory originated from the Father. His ultimate desire was that all would come to know the Father and he would do his part for those God had had placed in his surroundings would know God through him. Lastly, he desired that we all would be one with Him and the Father, just as he walked in oneness of mind, spirit and purpose!

Can you see the significant difference of a stance of sonship versus the other realms? This realm is a place of full security, authority, and power from a relationship that is not hesitant, double-minded, fearful, intimidated, or distant. Sons have such familiarity, assurance, confidence and knowledge of their Father and their assignment that their prayers are always attached to purpose and never in reflection of themselves but always in the image of their Father. Sons are not afraid to ask for glory. Sons are not afraid to operate in power, although they may choose not to (as when Jesus was tempted by Satan), because they are able to discern their time as given to them by the Father. Sons are clear on what they have been called to do and will not apologize for their assignment or authority, and remain aware of their responsibility to continually reflect the image of their Father to others, as the ultimate goals is for all to know Him.

Most of us have not advanced to this dimension. The bible lets us know that this is the place of perennial power that we as the body have yet to achieve. How do we know this? Because Romans 8:19 says "the earth is groaning for the manifestation of the sons of God". It is not until we can arise to this dimension that we really have the ability to literally and figuratively change the earth. The earth is waiting for true sons to take their position, authority and power as sons and operate in the fullness of God's spirit and one with both the Father and the Son.

"Father, we desire to be one with you and our Lord and Savior Jesus Christ. Teach us by your spirit, how to be one with you. Sanctify us by the truth of your word. Help us to be brought to

complete unity with you and one another. Protect us from the evil one, and teach us how to operate solely and completely from the realm of your purpose, your image, and your glory.

Let us all purpose to satisfy the longing of the earth and press on to the mark of the high calling of sonship, and facilitate our dominion in the earth!

CHAPTER SEVEN
TALKING WITH GOD

Now that we have taken a look at the postures of communication of some of our forefathers, let's take a closer look at the pattern of communication with God and man, beginning with Adam, before the fall. We always can look to the garden before the fall to receive enlightenment of God's intentions for man before sin entered in. We can see the order of marriage, the assignments he gave Adam, the ecological system he had in place and the functionality and purpose of all things…

Genesis 2:7-19

7And the LORD God formed man of the dust of the ground, and breathed into his nostrils the breath of life; and man became a living soul. 8And the LORD God planted a garden eastward in Eden; and there he put the man whom he had formed. 9And out of the ground made the LORD God to grow every tree that is pleasant to the sight, and good for food; the tree of life also in the midst of the garden, and the tree of knowledge of good and evil. 10And a river went out of Eden to water the garden; and from thence it was parted, and became into four heads. 11The name of the first is Pison: that is it which compasseth the whole land of Havilah, where there is gold; 12And the gold of that land is good: there is bdellium and the onyx stone. 13And the name of the second river is Gihon: the same is it that compasseth the whole land of Ethiopia. 14And the name of the third river is Hiddekel: that is it which goeth toward the east of Assyria. And the fourth river is Euphrates. 15And the LORD God took the man, and put him into the garden of Eden to dress it and to keep it. 16And the LORD God commanded the man, saying, Of every tree of the garden thou mayest freely eat: 17But of the tree of the knowledge of good and evil, thou shalt not eat of it: for in the day that thou eatest thereof thou shalt surely die. 18And the LORD God said, It is not good that the man should be alone; I will make him an help meet for him. 19And out of the ground the LORD God formed every beast of the field, and every fowl of the air; and brought them unto Adam to see what he would call them: and whatsoever Adam called every living creature, that was the name thereof.

We see that in the pure state of oneness with God, He did not dictate to Adam every instruction, but because the Spirit of the creator was so alive and sharpened within Adam, when Adam opened his mouth to "call" the hither fore unnamed animal, what Adam called it, **"it was"** what God had already named it. It WAS its name, it did not become its we often spend years, and some even a lifetime not knowing our purpose, not understanding our authority, and having no dominion? Because we have not entered into this dimension of relationship where God speaks to us face to face, does not hold anything back from us, and where we are assured of His presence, His purpose, and His power being the center of our being.

As we begin to seek God, armed with the "remembrance of His word", and we ask the Holy Spirit to show us how to be one with the sprit, and how to raise our children to honor, discern, and protect His presence, we will eliminate wasted years, unfruitful efforts, and untold frustrations that result from us not being in alignment with God's original purpose and plan for our lives.

God, help me to get to the place where we are one, so that when I open my mouth, what comes out is what already "was". I give you permission to circumcise my heart and my spirit so that they will be in alignment with your original intentions for me. I desire to live such a natural life in your spirit that I am always assured that what I speak and say is inspired by you. I thank you for

revealing to me once again, your purpose, assuring me of your presence, and trusting me with your power to be a witness to all of the earth. Holy Spirit, teach me how to communicate with God, from the place of God's original intention, in oneness of mind, spirit, soul, and body.

Let's revisit Cain once again to clearly observe God's conversation with Cain, even after the entrance of sin, God still attempted to guide and direct:

Genesis 4:2-16

2And she again bare his brother Abel. And Abel was a keeper of sheep, but Cain was a tiller of the ground. 3And in process of time it came to pass, that Cain brought of the fruit of the ground an offering unto the LORD. 4And Abel, he also brought of the firstlings of his flock and of the fat thereof. And the LORD had respect unto Abel and to his offering: 5But unto Cain and to his offering he had not respect. And Cain was very wroth, and his countenance fell. 6And the LORD said unto Cain, Why art thou wroth? and why is thy countenance fallen? 7If thou doest well, shalt thou not be accepted? and if thou doest not well, sin lieth at the door. And unto thee shall be his desire, and thou shalt rule over him. 8And Cain talked with Abel his brother: and it came to pass, when they were in the field, that Cain rose up against Abel his brother, and slew him. 9And the LORD said unto

Cain, Where is Abel thy brother? And he said, I know not: Am I my brother's keeper? 10And he said, What hast thou done? the voice of thy brother's blood crieth unto me from the ground. 11And now art thou cursed from the earth, which hath opened her mouth to receive thy brother's blood from thy hand; 12When thou tillest the ground, it shall not henceforth yield unto thee her strength; a fugitive and a vagabond shalt thou be in the earth. 13And Cain said unto the LORD, My punishment is greater than I can bear. 14Behold, thou hast driven me out this day from the face of the earth; and from thy face shall I be hid; and I shall be a fugitive and a vagabond in the earth; and it shall come to pass, that every one that findeth me shall slay me. 15And the LORD said unto him, Therefore whosoever slayeth Cain, vengeance shall be taken on him sevenfold. And the LORD set a mark upon Cain, lest any finding him should kill him. 16And Cain went out from the presence of the LORD, and dwelt in the land of Nod, on the east of Eden.

So now, we see even after the entrance of sin, although God had banished Adam and his family from the Garden of Eden, God, in his love and mercy, still communicated with this family as noted by his direct dialogue with Cain. In the passage above, God addressed Cain's countenance, his attitude, and his disposition. God gave him a warning that sin was still yet an option, it was "desiring" him, but he let Cain know that he could "rule" over it! That is what our loving, merciful God does every day of our lives if we would just stop and open our ears to hear the warnings that God is whispering to help us avoid every demonic force that "desires" us. Even though Cain, unlike his parents was "born in sin" and "shaped in iniquity" God still talked with him and they conversed, not as a formality, but conversationally, naturally and poignantly, with Cain expressing himself truthfully and at times, as in the case of God's warning, not responding at all. We can see clearly that the exchange between God and man was not a planned, repetitious, formula driven encounter, but a natural conversation between the creator and His creation. We also learn from this passage that God, even though we are no longer in the perfect state that he made us, attempts to warn us because of his great love and great mercy that he has towards us.

God, help me to discern every demonic spirit that is lying in wait for us and for our family. We denounce every spirit that is not of you and we rely on the power of the Holy Spirit that has given us the ability and the authority to tread upon every serpent and to bind up every attack of the enemy. We know our heritage as children of God is that "no weapon formed against us shall prosper" and we expose the enemy with the light of your word

and obliterate this attack and render it powerless in Jesus' name. Lord give me an ear that I will hear what your spirit is saying. I promise that as I hear your voice, I will not harden my heart, but I will obey and I will rule over every sin that desires me. Teach me how to talk with you in honesty and truthfulness concerning all of my struggles and even the sin that I know are at my door. I will not hesitate to talk with you, even when I am angry, frustrated, busy, confused or discouraged because I recognize that it is from your presence that I will receive joy, strength, encouragement, and direction. Thank you, Lord, that I am not bound by any methods or formulas in talking to you, but that even when I sin, I have access through repentance and I can expect you to guide me and direct me knowing that your desire is that no sin will rule over me. Lord, I thank you that from this day on, I will talk with you, without hesitation or reservations, but in humility of heart, simplicity of speech, and with a listening ear to receive your instructions, hear your rebukes, honor your commands and to bask in the security of your voice.

(Now just take some time to talk to God in your own words, allowing Him to reveal to you any sin, and expressing to him your true feelings with no hesitations or fear)

CHAPTER EIGHT
WALKING WITH GOD

The next exchange we see between God and man is with Noah. The bible says that "Noah was a righteous man, blameless among the people of his time, and **he walked with God.**" So, like Adam, who walked with God in the cool of the day, we see that there was a special relationship with those who walked with God. Enoch walked with God; Noah walked with God. Some of the most noted forefathers did not just serve God, they did not just know God, they did not even just worship God, or just talk with him, they **walked** with God.

What does it mean to walk with God? Let's start with Amos 3:3, which actually takes a look at the beginning point of our "walk" with God:

Amos 3:3 Can two walk together except they be agreed?

Our walk with God commences when we agree

with him. When we agree that Jesus Christ is our Lord and Savior who died for us and for the sins of the world, then our walk with the Lord begins. Every revelation of agreement translates to another spiritual "step" as we come to know him and the power of his resurrection. When we discover and agree that His word is the ultimate source of truth, we take another step. When we are in agreement with all of his commands and decrees, each act of obedience is a "step" on this path so the more we obey Him, His word and His spirit, the further we progress in our walk.

The failure to agree, and thus obey stagnates our walk with God. This is why there are many who remain "babes" in Christ or to put it another way, or have not gone far. Failure to take the steps of obedience in loving our neighbor as ourselves, or putting a guard over our tongues, or preferring others over ourselves, will cause us to stay in the same place, and therefore not progress and not "walk" with God. Paul put it this way, in Galatians 5:25 he said, "If we live in the Spirit, let us also **walk** in the Spirit". So, this verse literally means if we live in the Spirit (are alive, alert, and aware of the spirit) then let us also conform to or obey the Spirit to which we have been awakened. Many Christians have been awakened to the Spirit of God but have not gotten to the place of conforming to the Spirit of God and His likeness. Thus, our walk cannot begin without this total agreement. Disobedience and lack of agreement place us on a spiritual treadmill, where we can be having a lot of activity, and mimicking the sweat and toil of the kingdom, but failing to really be going anywhere.

Have you ever felt that you have put in a lot of work, time, and effort but you look up and see you are in the same place? Make sure that you have truly been "walking" with God. John Gill's Exposition of the bible gives a powerful explanation of how crucial it is for us to ensure we are walking in the spirit and not just living in the Spirit:

(Commentaries - John Gill's Exposition of the Bible - Old Testament)

Amos 3:3 Can two walk together except they be agreed?

Unless they meet together, and appoint time and place, when and where they shall set out, what road they will take, and whither they will go; **without such consultation and agreement, it cannot be thought they should walk together;** and not amicably, unless united in friendship, and are of the same affection to each other, and of the same sentiments one with another; or it is much if they do not fall out by the way. The design of these words is to show, that **without friendship there is no fellowship,** and without concord no communion; as this is the case between man and man, so between God and man; and that Israel could not expect that God should walk with them, and show himself friendly to them, and continue his favors with them, when they walked contrary to him; when they were so disagreeable to him in their sentiments of religion, in their worship, and the rites of it, and in the whole of their conduct and behavior. And **to a spiritual walk with God, and communion with him, agreement is requisite.** God and man were originally chief friends, but sin set them at variance; a reconciliation became necessary to their walking together again; which was set on foot, not by man, who had no inclination to it, nor knew how to go about it if he had, and much less able to effect it; but by the Lord, the offended party: it began in his thoughts, which were thoughts of peace; it was set on foot by him in the council of peace, and concluded in the covenant of peace; and his Son was sent to bring it about; and through his obedience, sufferings, and death, through his sacrifice and satisfaction, the agreement is made on the part of God, his justice is satisfied; but still it is necessary man should be agreed too; this is brought out by the Spirit of God, who shows the sinner the enmity of his mind, the sin and danger of it, slays this enmity, and puts in new principles of light, life, and love; when the soul is reconciled to God's way of salvation, and loves the Lord, and delights in him;

and both being thus agreed, the one by the satisfaction of Christ, and the other by the Spirit of Christ, see (Romans 5:10) ; they walk comfortably together: the saint walks with God, not only as in his sight and presence, but by faith, and in his fear, in the ways and ordinances of the Lord; and particularly is frequent in prayer and meditation, in which much of his walk with God lies: and God walks with him; he grants his gracious presence; manifests his love and favor to him; talks with him by the way; discloses the secrets of his heart; and indulges him with nearness and communion with him; but all is founded on mutual agreement.

So, as we take the first step of the beginning of our walk with God by accepting his son as Lord and Savior, we become in agreement with Jesus as our Lord when we also accept his word as the ultimate truth. Additionally, when we accept Jesus as Lord, we also accept Jehovah as Father and the Holy Spirit as our comforter and guide. This is the "appointed time and place" where our walk with the Lord begins. This is the place where we turn over our lives to God, and accept his path and his purposes. We are then only to be led down the path of righteousness, guided by his spirit and in acceptance of all of the twists, turns, valleys and hills that our walk with God takes us. Knowing that goodness and mercy is following us on this path, we don't have to look back but only pressing forward to the mark of the high calling in Christ Jesus!

One of the most difficult things we face as Christians is to continue as we began our walk---- in faith, love, obedience, thankfulness, prayer, and complete hope and trust in God's mercy, favor and grace! I believe this is what separated Enoch from others that God was so pleased with him! Enoch walked **with God** at a level that was obviously exceptional. However, this accomplishment was not because of personality or any superhuman capabilities, but for over 300 years he walked with God, in faith, trusting him, following him, and being in total agreement with God, with no controversy about who was in charge, but maintaining communion, fellowship, friendship, and sonship at a level that so pleased God that he honored him by allowing him to escape death!

You will see when you study closely the lives of our Forefathers, like Abraham and Noah, that there is more recorded in the scriptures about what God spoke to them, as opposed to what they spoke to God! I challenge you to study the lives of those God entrusted and made covenants with and you will see that he did most of the talking! This seems to be an implication that those who walk closer to God do more listening than talking. Prayer, as we know it, is hard to find in the scriptures of those like Noah who was found "perfect" in his generation. What we find is that God was pleased with his life, which resulted in Him giving Noah instructions that he quickly obeyed. What is revealed in scripture concerning God's communication with many of our patriarchs is perpetual conversation between them and God where God speaks, and they obey!

Father, teach me how to walk in the spirit through perpetual obedience and agreement to your will and your word. Father I desire for the pace of my walk to be accelerated through the immediacy of my obedience to pray, forgive, deny myself, love, and serve others over myself. Teach me how to walk with you even as our forefathers walked with you, help me by your spirit to reconcile every area in my life, thoughts, or behavior that has hindered my walk with you. I now give your word the ultimate authority in my life to align everything and everyone connected to me to be in agreement with your will, your purpose, and your plan.

CHAPTER NINE THE GOD OF OUR FATHERS

Now that we have determined what prayer is, the postures of prayer, and the importance of walking with God. Let's begin our journey of "looking back" to the rock from which we have come from, the patterns of our forefathers and get a different perspective on how to talk with our Father. The prayers of our fathers were effective for them, and as we pray in faith believing, equipped with understanding, they will be effective for us also. These prayers are just the beginning for you to learn how the patriarchs communed with God. Soon, you will have your own prayers and your own special language in speaking with your heavenly Father. Begin to pray these prayers and watch God reveal himself to you in ways like never before. I trust that you will see the simplicity, sincerity, and sanctification of our Father's prayers, as being the key ingredient to their effectiveness. May God bless you as we stand in agreement with our forefathers, activating their promises that are still applicable to us. May you also always remember God the way that he requested, as the God of Abraham, Isaac, and Jacob.

And God said moreover unto Moses, Thus shalt thou say unto the children of Israel, the LORD God of your fathers, the God of Abraham, the God of Isaac, and the God of Jacob, hath sent me unto you: this is my name for ever, and this is my memorial unto all generations.

Exodus 3:15

CHAPTER TEN THE PRAYERS OF THE PATRIARCHS

Following are the prayers that our Fathers prayed, directly to our heavenly Father, adjusted for us to pray them to Him today, in the spirit of our forefathers and in agreement with their prayers. Knowing that we are the seed of Abraham, we can pray according to faith and with "so great a cloud of witnesses" in agreement because their prayers are eternal. This volume covers selected prayers that date from the beginning until the time of Solomon. They appear in chronological order, and not surprisingly, cover many of the same issues of life that we have today…Please note that our "forefathers" include both men and women, denoting our entire spiritual heritage that has gone before us.

As you become familiar with these prayers you may select one or two to meditate daily on, based on your need at the moment. You will see from these prayers that when our forefathers needed something from God, many times they asked a question – and God gave them an answer. Prepare your spirit to begin to pray with simplicity, sincerity and with a sanctified lifestyle and you will see the same results as you pray THE PRAYERS OF the patriarchs.

THE PRAYERS OF ISAAC

May God give me of the dew of heaven, and the fatness of the earth, and the plenty of corn and wine. (Gen 27:28)

May God bless me, and make me fruitful, and multiply me, and give the blessing of Abraham to me, and to my seed with me; that I will inherit the land. (Gen 28 3-4)

THE PRAYERS OF MOSES:

I will sing unto the Lord, for he is highly exalted. The Lord is my strength and my song; he has become my salvation. He is my God, and I will praise him, my father's God, and I will exalt him. The Lord is a warrior; the Lord is his name. Your right hand is majestic in power. Your right hand shatters the enemy. In the greatness of your majesty you throw down those who oppose you. The enemy boasts, but you blow your breath and they are destroyed. Who is like you, Lord? Who is like you---majestic in holiness, awesome in glory, and working wonders?

The Prayers of the Patriarchs

In your unfailing love you will lead the people you have redeemed. In your strength you will guide them to your holy dwelling. The nations will hear and tremble. The chiefs will be seized with trembling. You will plant your people on the mountain of your inheritance---the place, O Lord, you made for your dwelling, the sanctuary, O Lord, your hands established. You, O Lord, will reign for ever and ever. (Ex 15:1-18)

Lord, why should your anger burn against your people, whom you have delivered with a mighty hand? Why should the heathen say that you brought us out just to kill us? Turn from your fierce anger; relent and do not bring disaster on your people. Remember your servants Abraham, Isaac and Israel, to whom you swore by your own self: "I will make your descendants as numerous as the stars in the sky and I will give your descendants all this land I promised them, and it will be their inheritance forever." (Ex 32:11-14)

You have told me to lead your people, I know you by name and you have found favor with me. If you are pleased with me, teach me your ways so that I may know you and continue to find favor with you. Remember that this nation is your people. (Ex 33:12-13)

If your presence does not go with me, do not send

me. How else will anyone know that you are pleased with me unless you go with me? What else will distinguish me and your people from all other people on the face of the earth? (Ex 33:15-16)

Show me your glory. (Ex 33:18)

O Lord, the compassionate and gracious God, slow to anger, abounding in love and faithfulness, maintaining love to thousands, and forgiving wickedness, rebellion and sin. Yet, you do not leave the guilty unpunished; you punish the children and their children for the sin of the fathers to the third and fourth generation. (Ex 34:6-7)

Lord, if I have found favor in your eyes, then go with me. Forgive our wickedness and our sin, and take us as your inheritance. (Ex 34:9)

Why have you brought this trouble on your servant? What have I done to displease you? I cannot carry this burden; it is too heavy for me. If I have found favor in your eyes, do not let me face my own ruin. (Num 11: 11-15)

By your power you have have brought us out. Now may your strength be displayed, just as you have declared: You are slow to anger, abounding in love and forgiving sin and rebellion. In accordance with your great love, forgive the sin of your people, just as you have pardoned before. (Num 14:13-20).

May the Lord, the God of the spirits of all mankind, appoint a man over this community to go out and come in before them, one who will lead them out and bring them in, so the Lord's people will not be like sheep without a shepherd. (Num 27:15-27)

May the Lord, the God of our fathers, increase us a thousand times and bless us as he has promised! (Deut 1:11)

Help me to be careful to do what you have commanded and not turn aside to the right or to the left. Teach me how to walk in all the way that you have commanded so that I may live and prosper and prolong my days in the land that I will possess. (Deut 5:32-33)

When you bring me into the land you swore to our fathers, cities I did not build, houses with all kinds of good things I did not provide, wells I did not dig, and vineyards and groves I did not plant--- when I eat and am satisfied help me to be careful that I do not forget you, my Lord and my God. (Deut 6:10-13)

The Lord bless you and keep you; the Lord make his face shine upon you and be gracious to you; the Lord turn his face toward you and give you peace. (Num 6:22-26)

Listen, O heavens, and I will speak; hear, O earth, the words of my mouth. Let my teaching fall like rain and my words descend like dew, like showers on new grass, like abundant rain on tender plants. I will proclaim the name of the Lord. Oh, praise the greatness our God! He is the Rock, his works are perfect, and all his ways are just. A faithful God who does no wrong, upright and just is he. (Deut 33:1-4)

The Lord will judge his people and have compassion on his servants, he will take vengeance on his enemies and make atonement for his land and people. (Deut 32:36,43)

The prayers of joshua

What message does the Lord have for his servant? (Josh 5:14)

What will you do for your own great name? (Josh 7:9)

The prayer of manoah

Let the men and women of God you have sent to us, teach us how to bring up our children. (Jud 13:8)

THE PRAYER OF SAMPSON

O Sovereign Lord, remember me. Please strengthen me once again. (Jud 16:28)

THE PRAYER OF THE SONS OF ISREAL

Shall we go up again for this battle? (Jud 20:23)

THE PRAYER OF THE MEN OF ISREAL

O God of Israel, why should one of us be missing from the kingdom? (Jud 21:2-3)

THE PRAYERS OF HANNAH

O Lord Almighty, if you will only look upon your servant's misery and remember me and not forget your servant. (1 Sam 1:11)

My heart rejoices in the Lord; in the Lord my horn is lifted high. My mouth boasts over my enemies, for I delight in your deliverance. There is no one holy like you Lord; there is no one besides you; there is no Rock like our God. (1 Sam 2:1-2)

Help me not to talk proudly or let my mouth speak or let my mouth speak such arrogance, for the Lord is a God who knows, and by him deeds are weighed. (I Sam 2:3)

The Lord humbles and exalts. He raises the poor from the dust and the needy from the ash heap; he seats them with princes and has them inherit a throne of honor. For the foundations of the earth are the Lord's;

upon them he has set the world. He will guard the feet of his saints, but the wicked will be silenced in darkness. It is not by strength that one prevails; those who oppose the Lord will be shattered. He will thunder against them from heaven; the Lord will judge the ends of the earth. He will give strength to his king and exalt the horn of his anointed. (1 Sam 2:6-10)

THE PRAYER OF SAMUEL

Lord speak for your servant is listening (1 Sam 3:10)

THE PRAYER OF SAUL

God of Israel, Give me the right answer (1 Sam 14:41)

THE PRAYERS OF DAVID

Deliver me from my enemies, O God; protect me from those who want to destroy me. Deliver me from evildoers and save me from murders. (Ps 59:1,2)

Be merciful to me, for all day I am pursued and attacked. When I'm afraid, I will trust in You, I will praise Your Word. As I trust in You, I will not be afraid (Ps 56:1,2)

I am under your promises Oh God and am thanking you with all my heart. You God have delivered me from death; you have kept my feet from stumbling so that I may walk before You. (Ps 56:12,13)

Lord, I bless you all time; my praise to you will always flow from my mouth. My soul boasts of God so the afflicted can hear and rejoice. Oh magnify the Lord with me; let us exalt His name together. I sought You Lord, and You answered me; delivered me from all my fears. As I look at You, my face is radiant and covered no more with shame. (Ps 34:1,2)

When I had nothing, you heard me and saved me from all my troubles. Angel of the Lord, encamp around me and deliver me. I've experienced you and have seen your goodness. As I take refuge in You, I am blessed. As I continue to Fear You, I will lack nothing; as I seek You, I will lack no good thing. (Ps 34:8-10)

Your eyes are on the righteous and Your ears are attentive to our cry; Your face is against those who do evil so the memory of them is cut form the earth. As I cry to You, You hear me and deliver me from my troubles. When my heart is broken you are close; when my spirit is crushed, you are there to save me. (Ps 34:15-17)

Though I have many troubles, You God deliver me from all of them – even guarding my bones. Evil shall destroy the wicked, those who hate the righteous will be condemned, but the Lord redeems the soul of His servants. (Ps 34:18-22)

I cry loud to You; I lift up my voice to for mercy; I pour out my complaints; I tell you all my problems. When I get tired it is you who know how I'm feeling. (Ps 142:1-3)

No matter where I look, no one is concerned for me; no one cares for my life. So I cry to you Lord. You are my refuge – my only hope for life. Listen to my cry, for I am in desperate need. Rescue me from those who pursue me, for they are too strong for me. Set me free from this prison so I may praise

Your Name. (Ps 142:4-7)

God, you are my God. Earnestly I seek you. My soul thirsts for you, my body longs for you. I've seen you in the sanctuary; I've seen Your Power and Your Glory. Your Love is better than LIFE. As long as I live, my lips will glorify you and I will lift up my hands to praise you. With songs I will praise you. (Ps 63:1-5)

Save Me. Vindicate Me. Hear my prayer. Listen to Me. Strangers are attacking me; ruthless men with no regard for You are seeking my life. God, You are my Help; You are the one that sustains me. In your faithfulness destroy those who slander me. Willingly, I will sacrifice an offering to you. I praise your name, O Lord, for you are good. You delivered me from all my troubles and my eyes saw my enemies defeated. (Ps 54)

Shall I pursuit this battle? Will I win? (1 Sam 30:7)

Shall I go and attack? Will you hand them over to me? (2 Sam 5:19)

Lord, my Strength, I Love You. You are my rock, my fortress, my deliverer, my shield, my salvation and my stronghold in which I take refuge. I all to you because you are worthy of praise and I am saved from my enemies. (Ps 18:1-3)

Lord, you reached down from Heaven and took hold of me; you drew me out of deep waters. You rescued me from my powerful enemy, my foes that were too strong for me. When my enemies confronted me in the day of my disaster, You Lord was my support. You brought me out and you rescued me because you delighted in me. (Ps 18:16-19)

The Lord has rewarded me according to my righteousness and cleanness of my hands. I have kept the ways of the Lord; I have not turned from God; I have not turned away from God's decrees. I have been blameless and have kept myself from sin. (Ps 18:20-22)

To the faithful you show yourself faithful, to the

blameless you show yourself blameless, to the pure you show yourself pure, but to the crooked you show yourself shrewd. You save the humble, but your eyes are on the prideful to bring them low. You are my light, O Lord; the Lord turns my darkness into light. With your help I can advance against a troop; with You God, I can scale a wall. (Ps 18:25-29)

God's way is perfect; His Word is flawless. He is a shield for all who take refuge in him. Who is God besides the Lord? Who is the Rock except our God? (Ps 18:30,31)

God arms me with strength and makes my way perfect. God makes my feet like the feet of a deer; enabling me to stand on the heights. God trains my hands for battle; my arms to bend a bow of bronze. God give me your shield of victory, sustain me you're your right hand, stoop down to make me great; broaden the path beneath me, so my ankles do not turn. (Ps 18:32-36)

God has delivered me from the attacks of people; You made me the head of nations; people I do not know are subject to me. When they hear me, they obey me; foreigners cringe before me; they lose heart; they come trembling from their strongholds. The Lord lives! I exalt God my Savior. He is the God who avenges me, who saves me from my enemies. He is the God who exalted me above my enemies; He is the God who rescued me from violent men. Therefore I will praise him among the nations; I will sing praises to Your Name. (Ps 18:43-49)

Give thanks to the Lord, call on his name; make known among the nations what he has done. Sing to him, sing praise to him; tell of all his wonderful acts. Glory in his holy name; let the hearts of those who seek the Lord rejoice. Look to the Lord and his strength; seek his face always. Remember the wonders he has done, his miracles, and the judgment he pronounced. (Ps 105:1-5)

"Who am I, LORD, and what is my family, that you have brought me this far? And as if this were not enough in your sight, you have also spoken about the future of my family. Is this your usual way of dealing with man? "What more can I say to you? For you know your servant. For the sake of your word and according to your will, you have done this great thing and made it known to your servant. "How great you are, O Sovereign LORD! There is no one like you, and there is no You have established your people Israel as your very own forever, and you, O LORD, have become their God. "And now, LORD God, keep forever the promise you have made concerning my house. Do as you promised, so that your name will be great forever. Then men will say, 'The LORD Almighty is God over Israel!' And the house of your servant David will be established before you. "O

LORD Almighty, God of Israel, you have revealed this to your servant, saying, 'I will build a house for you.' So your servant has found courage to offer you this prayer. O Sovereign LORD, you are God! Your words are trustworthy, and you have promised these good things to your servant. Now be pleased to bless my house, that it may continue forever in your sight; for you, O Sovereign LORD, have spoken, and with your blessing the house of your servant will be blessed forever." (2 Sam 7:18-29)

Have mercy on me, O God, according to your unfailing love; according to your great compassion blot out my transgressions. Wash away all my iniquity and cleanse me from my sin. For I know my transgressions, and my sin is always before me. Against you, you only, have I sinned and done what is evil in your sight, so that you are proved right when you speak and justified when you judge. Surely, I was sinful at birth. Cleanse me with hyssop, and I will be clean; wash me, and I will be whiter than snow. Let me hear joy and gladness; let the bones you have crushed rejoice. Hide your face from my sins and blot out all my iniquity. Create in me a pure heart, O God, and renew a steadfast spirit within me. Do not cast me from your presence or take your Holy Spirit from me. Restore to me the joy of your salvation and grant me a willing spirit, to sustain me. In your good pleasure make Zion prosper; build up the walls of Jerusalem. Then there will be righteous sacrifices, whole burnt offerings to delight you; then bulls will be offered on your altar. (Ps 51:1-5,7-12,18,19)

You are a shield around me, Lord; you bestow glory on me and lift up my head. I cry aloud, and You answer me from your holy hill. I lie down and sleep; I wake again, because the Lord sustains me. I will not fear the tens of thousands drawn against me. Arise, O Lord! Deliver me, strike all my enemies. Deliverance comes form you; may your blessing be on your people (Ps 3:3-7)

I have sinned greatly in what I've done. Take away my guilt. I have done a very foolish thing. (2 Sam 24:10)

I will exalt you, O Lord, for you lifted me out of the depths and did not let my enemies gloat over me. O Lord my God, I called to you for help and you healed me. You brought me up from the grave; you spared me from going down into the pit. (Ps 30:1-3)

The prayers of solomon

I am but a little child; I know not how to go out or come in. Your servant is in the middle of great people you have chosen. Therefore, give me an understanding heart to judge your people that I may be able to discern between good and evil. (1 Kings 3:7-9)

"O LORD, God of Israel, there is no God like you in heaven above or on earth below—you who keep your covenant of love with your servants who continue wholeheartedly in your way. You have kept your promise. With your mouth you have promised and with your hand you have fulfilled it—as it is today. And now, O God of Israel let your word that you promised come true. (1 Kngs 8:22-26)

"When a man wrongs his neighbor and is required to take an oath and he comes and swears the oath before you, then hear from heaven and act. Judge between your servants, condemning the guilty and bringing down on his own head what he has done. Declare the innocent not guilty, and so establish his innocence. (1 Kngs 8:31,32)

"When your people have been defeated by an enemy because they have sinned against you, and when they turn back to you and confess your name, praying and making supplication to you, then hear from heaven and forgive the sin of your people and bring them back to the land you gave to their fathers. (1 Kngs 8:33,34)

"When the heavens are shut up and there is no rain because your people have sinned against you, and when they pray and confess your name and turn from their sin because you have afflicted them, then hear from heaven and forgive the sin of your servants, your people. Teach them the right way to live, and send rain on the land you gave your people for an inheritance. (1 Kngs 8:35,36)

"When famine or plague comes to the land, or blight or mildew, locusts or grasshoppers, or when an enemy besieges them in any of their cities, whatever disaster or disease may come, and when a prayer or plea is made by any of your people Israel—each one aware of the afflictions of his own heart, and spreading out his hands toward you - then hear from heaven, your dwelling place. Forgive and act; deal with each man according to all he does, since you know his heart (for you alone know the hearts of all men); so that they will fear you all the time they live in the land you gave our fathers. (1 Kngs 8:37-40)

"As for the foreigner who does not belong to your people Israel but has come from a distant land because of your name- for men will hear of your great name and your mighty hand and your outstretched arm—when he comes and prays toward you, then hear from heaven, your dwelling place, and do whatever the foreigner asks of you, so that all the peoples of the earth may know your name and fear you, as do your own people Israel, and may know that this house I have built bears your Name. (1 Kngs 8:41-43)

"When your people go to war against their

enemies, wherever you send them, and when they pray to the LORD toward the city you have chosen and the temple I have built for your Name, then hear from heaven their prayer and their plea, and uphold their cause. (1 Kegs 8:44,45)

"Now, my God, may your eyes be open and your ears attentive to the prayers offered in this place." Now arise, O LORD God, and come to your resting place, you and the ark of your might. May your priests, O LORD God, be clothed with salvation, may your saints rejoice in your goodness. O LORD God do not reject your anointed one. Remember the great love promised to David your servant." (2 Chr 6:40-42)

ABOUT THE AUTHOR

Apostle Darlyn C. Turner has a vast arsenal of skills, abilities, and gifting. She is a producer, minister, coach, author, and leader of several organizations, including Billionaire Minds, a nonprofit organization dedicated to training and cultivating entrepreneurial skills and vision. Darlyn also recently founded The National Widows Association, a 501c3 organization dedicated to the advancement and empowerment of widows.

She now functions as the President of Holywood Studios, a Christian film and production company started by her late husband, Dr. Clifford E. Turner, the writer, producer, and director of the Emmy Award Winning series, The Awakening. She is the co-producer of the Women on the Move series, a nationally syndicated television series. Also, after the death of her husband, Darlyn became the President of The Liberty International Network, a collaborative of ministries, churches, businesses, and individuals dedicated to the advancement of the kingdom of God extending to all sectors of society. As a former executive of a Fortune 500 company, Darlyn has combined her experience, training, and skills to serve her community, mentor, and aid in the development of future leaders.

Apostle Darlyn's ultimate call and passion is to women and their empowerment. She has hosted several national women's conferences for over 20 years, and is a mentor to many women, helping them to fully embrace their identity, power, and purpose to fulfill their destinies and thrive mentally, physically, financially, and spiritually.

Apostle Darlyn's coaching, ministry, and expertise, which are timeless and genderless, transcend culture and lead to inner healing, personal empowerment, and success in life by opening both minds and hearts. Darlyn has made her mark in the municipalities, the marketplace and in ministry.

Darlyn resides in both the Chicagoland and Orlando areas. She currently has nine children and 4 grandchildren.

For more information about Apostle Darlyn you can visit her website at darlynturner.com or libertytemple.org.

www.ingramcontent.com/pod-product-compliance
Lightning Source LLC
Chambersburg PA
CBHW071316110426
42743CB00042B/2614